I0088373

HOLDING MYSELF HOSTAGE IN THE KITCHEN

CHICON
STREET
POETS
CHAP
BOOK
PRIZE
2017

DANIEL BLOKH

HOLDING MYSELF HOSTAGE IN THE KITCHEN

LIT CITY PRESS

Holding Myself Hostage In The Kitchen. Copyright © 2017. Daniel Blokh.

First Edition. All rights reserved.

No part of this book may be used or reproduced in any manner whatsoever without written permission except in the case of brief quotations embodied in critical articles and reviews.

For information about permissions to reproduce selections from this book, write to Lit City Press: hello@litcitypress.com.

Books may be purchased in quantity and / or special sales by contacting the publisher, Lit City Press: hello@litcitypress.com.

Published by Lit City Press / Lit City Publishing, Austin, Texas.

Cover and Interior Design by Lit City Press, Austin, Texas.

This publication is in conjunction with the Give Me Something Else chapbook poetry prize managed by the nonprofit literary arts organization Chicon Street Poets. The author, Daniel Blokh, is the recipient of the first prize, which entails publication of his work.

Chicon Street Poets is a nonprofit literary arts organization where writers can share and encourage the development of their craft, while engaging the community through poetry, arts enrichment services, and events. Lit City Press is a proud sponsor of this organization's ongoing monthly feature as well as the Give Me Something Else chapbook poetry prize. For more information:

www.chiconstpoets.com

Blokh, Daniel –

Holding Myself Hostage In The Kitchen : Poetry / American / General

ISBN-13: 978-0692959329 (Lit City Press / Lit City Publishing)
ISBN-10: 0692959327

Library of Congress Cataloging Number:

Lit City Press / Lit City Publishing

Austin, Texas

Printed in the United States of America

DEDICATION

для моего дома

CONTENTS

ACKNOWLEDGMENTS

Thank you to my friends, family, and colleagues for the unwavering support and for inclusion of the works in the following journals: *Herring*, in the Inquisitive Eater; *Icarus' Father Builds the Wings*, in the Blueshift Journal; *Erasing*, in Tenderness Yea; *Abecedarian for the English Language*, in Permafrost Magazine; *To the Toad I Hid in my Room for a Night*, in Susan / the Journal; *Dress-Up*, in KYSO Flash; *For a Better Self*, in Verdad; *Overeating*, in the Ellis Review; *To My First Language*, in the Foyle 2017 Commended Poets Anthology; *Muscle Memory*, in DIALOGIST.

INTRODUCTION

Is it possible to miss a life you know only by story? *holding myself hostage in the kitchen* is a deeply engaging narrative illuminating the poet's personal history as a first generation American, his family's Russian- Jewish heritage and history, home life, plain life, and modern life. With an observant eye, smart musical sense, and delightful craftsmanship, 16 year old Daniel Blokh delivers a mature meditation on identity. Perhaps it is possible to long for a life known only by story, and this collection pays homage to that space.

– **Nancy Lili Gonzalez**, *Foxing Quarterly*, *Round Top Poetry Anthology*, and *Sorin Oak Review.*

DANIEL BLOKH

Birdwatchers

though you're still too young
to remember your father
sits on the porch with you
to watch your first sundown

there is something burning
on the stove it is the first smell
you will later recognize
déjà vu of smoke playing

on the whistling wind your father
never noticing your father
too busy watching crows
fill the air a net

almost covering the sky
between each of them
he finds a space
to breathe through

RECIPES

DANIEL BLOKH

To Salt

This is how it happened: My mother
looking back at the city of her leaving, city

of her birth. You can run out of a burning
house and still turn back to see
your favorite birch tree one last time

so I was raised
by a pile of memories, learned early

to kneel near the lingering
of something I couldn't replace
no matter how many mountains built

on my back, how many forests
in my palms. This story holds happiness but

I'm not sure on which side. This happened
but I can't remember when. I can't know
where she looked back from,

if she saw the city in a plane's window, if
she found it folded in my eye.

Menu of a Childhood
after Amy Krouse Rosenthal

Item	Description	Price
Borscht	We had it almost every week. My brother and sister tried to cook it once. Turned out alright, but could never compare to my mother's years of practice.	$4.99
Wheat Thins	Breakfast when mother couldn't cook. Hated.	$3.39
Caviar	"A lot more expensive than in Russia," my mother laments.	$25.99
Chai	Good with small sweet snacks (see Pryaniki) in the presence of unfamiliar guests who my parents will speak of in the kitchen afterwards, with varying degrees of kindness.	$10.60
Pierogi	Mother made them to bring to school one day. Everyone said they looked good, but when I came back, half of them were left uneaten. Finished the rest off.	$7.85

Vodka	Always sat at the top of our kitchen cabinet. Once, when my parents were away, I got curious. Couldn't down more than one sip.	$20.00
Russian Honey Cake	Sweet, soft, perfect. Mother would only make it on special occasions, and we were always waiting.	$11.35
Pryaniki	Could only be purchased at a small, obscure grocery store. Snuck them into my room on sad nights.	$5.50
Steak	Friend's mother gave one to me when I visited his house. I smiled and thanked her when she set the plate down. My first time eating it. Everyone wolfed theirs down but I couldn't chew a bite. Spat it into a napkin when they weren't looking and ate potatoes until I lost my appetite.	$39.99

James Bond

screen flicks on / lights / camera another
commie / ka-plowed / to the jaw borscht
spilling from his unhinged tooth thick accent
sputtering / ka-plow
ka-plow / and my *mat* brings popcorn / a cup
of fresh *kvass* in / her hands / my *otets* smiles
because isn't it our agent 007 our rolling credits
our victory / our Sean Connery & Robert Shaw
/ & when the screen goes black / what can I do
but clap / clap / clap

Russian Alphabet

at two years old
my mother
makes me memorize it
turns me into a medium
waking a dead
home from her lips
bringing the country
of her birth
to life inside me
she's lived this way
since America carried
her belongings with her
in her children's faces
watched her homeland
ripple through their eyes
now she starts on me
working her country through
my mouth pulling
from my throat
her grandparents
her summer house
her nights in Moscow
they come out
in the shape of А
        Б
            В
               Г
                  Д
      she makes me start
        again again again
  I must know this language
        is never only mine
       it carries dead things
      long into the night
         mother knits

them into my mouth
turns my tongue to a river
painted in her blood
turns me into an echo
of the limbs she left
a continent away

**For My Late Great-Aunt
Deaf from Typhus Medication in WW2**

in your bed of old skins
your body lies snakelike

and cold/could have had a husband
to bring you

hot tea now/to hold you/could have been
married/happy/home

could have been/if not for the sick
spilling through your head

as the bullet through your neighbor's
the war hid blood in your ears

hid your body in dark corners
made you a burrow

out of cold and restless evenings
you made it through the fields

but they never made it through you
your ears left you and took with them

a hundred of your lives/killed
your past suitors/made future loves

too loud to live unheard/you curled
into yourself/shed possibility

after possibility/no life
could keep you long enough

I Will Invent a River

I have sat here in my stillness for a few hours

waiting is hard work

whatever the next step is it clings

with firm fists

like a baby reluctant for world

the clock ticks

the TV is playing

but I am not brave enough

to look away from the clock

I am waiting for the second motion

takes me through the door

through the streets of honking cars

cawing rubberneckers

I am waiting to ribbon all my possibilities

around the world

the version with a 4.0 GPA

the one that dies on Mars

all the ones

in between

and the moment

is on its way trust me

any second now

Herring

Cheap in the Soviet Union, Dedushka
would bring it for my mother to eat
with bread. Its salty skin could keep
his children full for days. In that time
- that country - herring flowed like rivers, fell
from the sky as snow, the whole Union
one big fish waiting to break away
into the ocean, swim to a better shore.

Some tastes hang inside a mouth for years
my mother says, fish frying on the pan
before her. Prices change, the mouth
too, but some flavors catch
your tongue. They keep you
company. They cross oceans
for you. They cross oceans.

Here Is Another Poem
In Which I've Let Myself Forget

even forgetting unlearned for a second
the inch of time the dead skin I hid in
like an overcoat in this poem I am not

growing I am not leaving anything only
picking up the leaves of a still tree
when this old oak dies I will not know

when the sun leaves us we won't notice
for a whole life, oops, I breathed
again, that was a record. last week

I threw out half my wardrobe, my body
lost too far into the world to fit a size
small shirt. "Who lived in you?" I asked

the fabric pile before I threw it out, "I don't
remember him - I think it hasn't been
so long since he was here, a lifetime."

Erasing

there was no stopping it the razor
a metal secret against my cheek
smooth steel appendage
in place of a guiding hand

I should have waited but you
were asleep and the window
caught my eye father I wanted to be clean
as the night sky I locked the door

looked in the moonlit glass
held the razor to my skin
wondering which way
the blade should go why
my cheeks seemed to sting

FILLINGS

DANIEL BLOKH

Icarus' Father Builds the Wings

Collecting feathers in the yard, he tells himself
each soft bird body

is only a harvest, a sprawl. He trims feather
from soft wing, down

from skin. He saws branches from trees, snaps
them, convinces himself

they will not be missed. In his eyes
they are not limbs. He takes them

to the kitchen, melts candles, smooths
the feathers over them. Outside, a sunny sky

hides storm. A bird sprawls
downwards, searches for its nest, finds air.

Abecedarian for the English Language

All day my mother lives inside
                a language she does not
Belong in. It loses her
                in hard ribs and
Cold vowels, in its dusty
                noise, its angles full of
Distance. Each morning, she tries to smooth
                out her tongue.
Each morning, she goes to the grocery store
                apologizes to the cashier
For her accent. *Escueeze me,* she says. *Imsorry.*
                She wants to say: *America*
Gave me home, but
                zis home
Had a price. She wants to say: *Imsorry*
                for my teeth.
Imsorry that I could not make
                zis language mine, zis
Jagged tongue. My mother's mouth
                was made for vowels
Knit from spice, sweat,
                sun. My mother carries
Languages that could melt
                snow, wake
Mountains from their cold white sleep.
                But my mother knows
No one can mispronounce silence.
                That she belongs
Only through closed teeth.
                With each year, she grows quieter.
Pale ice covers the rolling plains
                of her *r*s. She cannot
Quell this country's
                thirst. Back in

Russia, every voice was heavy
                 as hers. No one
Swallowed their tongue. But here, each evening
                 my mother asks me
To spellcheck her emails, to see
                 where she
Used past tense instead of present
                 misplaced a *The*, wrote
Vine for Wine. Each evening, the two of us
                 sit in the kitchen and play
Word games. When I win, she hugs me tight
                 eyes full of pride. *Danya*
Xenni etot yazik, she tells me.
                 Learn it vell.
You don't vant be like me. She wants
                 to say:
Zis language vaz never mine, but maybe can be yours.

To the Toad I Hid in my Room for a Night

My son, that evening, I imagined lifetimes
with you. My hands cold and unwashed
from carrying the wet green secret of you
left stains of dirt under my pillow.

I didn't notice. I drifted off, thinking

I heard you singing from the cramped shoebox
I turned into a home for you, stuffed with grass
and dirt. My son, I thought you could mistake
our house for a country, but maybe home

is easier said than done. Maybe the shoebox

had a hole. Maybe the holy hymnal sound
I heard was only the screen door squeaking
open, sound of your body lifting
as my mother lowered you to soft ground

sound of next morning's loss already creeping in.

Leaving A Scab Alone

time in your slow strut
    you take every bike ride
        out of me you take

the marks of wind the scratches
    on my knees
        their wild flush

you take the rush of color
    in each blue bruise
        my heart no longer

longs to peel a scab 13
    14   15   each year
        your countdown rips

the wind from me
    you take the air that held
        my voice above

the others lock me
    in my breath your kisses close
        my mouth

your touches heal the skin
        but keep the scratches in

Dress-Up

The way a shadow trying to forget itself
hides in light, my father steps

before a mirror and tries on this new
country. The house silent, the kids

hours from waking
and mistaking the beds beneath them

for their beds. My father slips
into the red-blue skin, zips up each stripe

and pretends he can breathe
through them. He poses, wonders

if this continent fits him
and if not, if he can fake it

well enough. The world

will see him in this outfit
and be proud, he thinks. Him

new man. Him, American. Not homesick
no commie.

Safe

i thought i was but the shower
water i spilled
               into convinced me

otherwise   every drop

pulled my skin further away
    the shower heard me but it wouldn't listen

i thought i was the boy
     i was   i told it

a boy my mother and father
could send safely into the world

in the mirror the fog wrote mercilessly
No   bliss never hides

in easy things   the way thirst is a guillotine
hidden   in the throat

the way things are what they are
until they aren't   i was until i wasn't
i sat down in the bath and asked

what am   i?

water shattered against the shower curtain.

every droplet said   *Yes.*

For a Better Self

where's your appetite gone? too far
to reach, i hope. i chop vegetables for you in the
kitchen, keep the stove going, lay out the table.
when i bring the knife down red shells part
before me, sweet and starved as mouths.

when the knife turns sideways i almost
see you in the glimmer, your thin body waiting
to become me. each metal click against
the wooden board counts a day
to your arrival. i keep my knife turned straight

wait to be split. i brush onions onto the pan.
i watch them turn perfect   swallowing light.

DANIEL BLOKH

BASIN

DANIEL BLOKH

On My Parents' Anniversary

I'm trying to take my time with everything
but it's difficult.

We're watching one of your favorite films, me
on the side of the table

 opposite the two of you; me looking at the
screen until not; until

I'm looking at my phone; me looking at my
phone until I'm reaching

for the pile of pumpkin seeds spread out
between us, tucking my teeth

behind a pale shell. A slow moment in the film
and I am far more interested

in scrolling through this article about salt, all
the ways it hunts us. I wolf

into another seed, throw it into the pile
of emptied *anyways*

given by a dying garden somewhere. I'm so far
into this article

I don't even slow to note the taste still
in my mouth. Did you know

all the terrible ways salt can kill?
It seems important

but you don't care, the two of you watching
this film lifted from your youth

trying to remember where you saw it, and
with who, and how many miles

away the theater. Or thinking
nothing at all. I slip

my greedy tongue into another seed
then realize I've had more

than both of you. I realize I'm sixteen years old
and there's enough salt in my throat

to bite away a lifetime. I look back
at the film.

I've missed the plot. The two of you
know it word for word

but you're leaning into the screen
and I don't want to crack

into this moment with a question. Someone says
a cool line; you both

laugh; you go for a seed at the exact same
time, slowly,

so slowly, your hands
brushing.

Surviving Summer

in the soft season boys lose
their bodies to something below
    the water this something gnaws

and tugs their skin
peels off in sweat
    no frantic doctor can bring it back

the soft season lingers
in reflections in bedsheets
    hides in some place

you'd never think of back of a throat
or a boy's palm
    it cannot be coaxed

out with scalpels
makes him feverish
    the doctor brings the bad news

to his parents wrapped in tissue paper
brings it gentle as a skin steeped in shower water
    as a tooth caught biting

Self Portrait as Sink

The sound of water washing you is the sound
of deep sighing, of stay here – the job interview
can wait, there are other trains. A stream
is only a stream until a hand moves through it.
Turn your palms up to receive. This softness
can cling in the air around you, even when water
becomes water again, when the door swings
open and shut. How grand it was when you
could climb onto the surface wash your feet
when you could dip your hair into that hollow
space and let it drip.

58

my father never
hunted once doesn't touch meat
lives softly enough to enter

> and leave the world a shadow
> a breeze on doorsteps
> he wakes at 3 am

just like his own father did wanders
the house a little pours his cereal
then reads the news until i wake

> on the ride to school he'll talk about
> the latest friend i didn't get to meet
> this one was only 52 and lived

back in kharkov they went to school
together sometimes my father asks
have you considered going vegetarian

> I say maybe which we both know

means I don't want to go to the trouble
of saying no

> we've made it to the school
> he hasn't had a chance
> to talk about the news

or ask my plans today
what is there to say but goodbye son
and goodbye

father   who is my son

whose face   I want to linger

in my memory whose eyes
I carry   with me
into any rear view mirror

watching the road behind me
yelling   honking
when one car sideswipes another

father who knows

            we live
            in a world

 of wheels
all trying to catch us

Overeating

Only because I want to be sure of my name.
Because this is what I will know when I know
nothing: the rice piled like mountains, bowls
of soy, pesto, sesame seeds. Even on holy days
I cannot bring myself to fast. I cannot face
the possibility of absence, how easily I could slip
out of myself. I sneak pierogi from the kitchen
swallow them in the bathroom, sweep
the crumbs. I carry my home inside me to always
remind myself what is holiest; to remember
the shape of my mother's fingers
in dough, the softness of the knife that carries
into butter, the butter onto bread, the smell
of it lingering heavy and real in the kitchen air.

9 Thoughts Of Home From 639 Miles Away

1.

If the oak shudders in wind
or only lets the memory of shuddering
pass through it, let me not think
about home.

2.

If the dark peering from behind its grey
bark looks familiar; if you smell a love song
if
green is the same everywhere; if green
is always the earth forgetting a dead body
or writing a poem about a dead body.

3.

Every ant folding under a shoe
is a frame, cold body opening
to let a thought rustle inside.

My mother will be
sixty this year.
I'll take a photo.

4.

One day I left my house to turn into
someone I love. When I came back
sixteen years had passed and
my dinner was cold.

5.

Vine   unconditionally

whether the tree breathes
or not, whether it is still alive
or hasn't known that name

in twenty years, the green
will still know nothing
but that body to love.

6.

Every forest is full of old forests
even if it doesn't know this yet.

Some things the body never leaves
until the body leaves.

7.

Even if time settles back into dirt; even if
every verb becomes a noun; if you become

an adult and forget
a name; if you forget many names

if the world can no longer be felt
oohing; if it no longer feels like

an endless familiar hand; if I'm only
telling myself this

so I can leave my house
in the morning.

8.

If   if   if   if   if   if.

9.

If an ant happens to crawl into
my hand, let him call me *mother*.

I Text My Dad *Shabbat Shalom!* 5000 Miles Away

And though this is a faux distance - summer
vacation for two weeks - I can already
feel my mind settling into this space yawning
in front of us. I'm looking at a college

in a small town too far north
to feel familiar, so it's time
for me and him to train, to learn speaking
through echoes of longer

words, to think of each other
when Friday evening comes, standing
over candles, the proper prayers turned rusty
in the back of our minds. We will fall asleep

knowing someone misses us. We will learn
to say all this across distance. The miles
will do their best to pass our messages
along. We will abbreviate our love to fit

5-minute phone calls, the candles
in our distant kitchens lit, yarmulkes
sitting on our bedside tables
as though watching.

Elegy to an Old Mother

Today I found a Russian lullaby
you sang when I was too young
to write poems or even fit
two languages into my brain

I still struggle; now I know
only half the words
I catch *My… fall… house…*
lights… faded… not enough

not held by you and rocked
in sleep's soft cloud
its imitation safety
in this recording

it's not your voice
shaking in melody
your voice was softer than
I knew a thing could be

it sat under the world
built a nest there
you sang and were 15
thinking home was a forever

then I had a birthday
and you had a birthday
and turned 50
and stopped singing.

Muscle Memory

Some things stay
forever in a body. The flavor
of an old fruit, or my father's humming
from the distant front seat
of his car. The color of a childhood
room, or the rearview mirror

where his eye glanced up for seconds
to see me. His voice a breeze
snuck through the cracked window.
Some things the body holds
dear. Others, it leaves
behind, how a voice
rises, an eye shakes. The body
drives past them.

I am at the wheel now, father, and the breeze
is humming outside the window.
On the road, the lines lie
like ribs. The sky is bright
as my old room, the one
you painted blue.

To My First Language

Old dog, I don't have time to take you
on walks anymore. I try to throw you bones
but you're a slow thing, heaving to my side
when I am lonely, low growl faltering.
My new dog comes at a finger's snap. He's cuter.
He has sharper teeth. He watches you
lumber through the yard and waits.

I wonder if one day he'll kill you
drag your body to my room
where I will try to mourn it, softly, slide
my hands through faded
fur. My parents taught me how to love you
so I could feed you when they left us.
They dreamed about the two of us alone
in this big house, this makeshift
model of a homeland, yard
where they pictured snow, imagined winters
coming over us, your body around mine
for heat.

DANIEL BLOKH

ABOUT THE AUTHOR

Daniel Blokh was the age of sixteen at the time of this publication. Blokh is an American writer of Russian-Jewish descent, living in Birmingham, Alabama. He is the author of the memoir *In Migration* (BAM! Publishing 2016), the micro-chapbook *The Wading Room* (Origami Poems Project 2016), and the chapbook *Grimmening* (forthcoming from Diode Editions). His work has been recognized by the Scholastic Art and Writing awards and Foyle Young Poet awards, and has appeared in *DIALOGIST*, *Permafrost*, *Blueshift*, *Cleaver*, *Gigantic Sequins*, *Forage Poetry*, *Avis*, *Thin Air*, and *Cicada*.

DANIEL BLOKH

www.ingramcontent.com/pod-product-compliance
Lightning Source LLC
Chambersburg PA
CBHW030154070426
42447CB00032B/1198

* 9 7 8 0 6 9 2 9 5 9 3 2 9 *